Local News

Poems
by
Sonja Margulies

Local News

Published by Sycamore Books
sycamore.books@gmail.com

Book design and layout by Amy Bradley, amybarrbradley@gmail.com

Cover painting by Miles Vich – "Ochre and yellow on black,"
gouache on paper, 8" x 9", 2009.
Miles Vich, PO Box 60488, Palo Alto, CA 94306

for Robin and Peter

Contents

Contents

Contents

Contents

Why Write

I never longed to be a poet.
I'm sure you can tell.
What poet would launch such
a frail and rough hewn craft
into the sea of literature
where it would surely sink
without a ripple.

Still, I write.
I write for friends.
I write to better know some
piece of life and tell it,
to read it back for truth,
to see if I have got it right,
to see if, after all is said
and done, repaired, reworked,
my boat, will float.

I
THE NOON WHISTLE

Remembering Childhood

As a child, lying on my back,
on the warm summer lawn
just after supper, at dusk,
I'd watch the feathered acrobats
flying so impossibly high,
darting, diving in the sky.
Barn swallows,
catching insects,
got their supper
on the fly.

A Reader's Way

I used to prop a book in the soap dish
while washing the dinner dishes
until Mother said that that was
going too far, and way beyond
proper attention to the task.
Not the right behavior.
So I stopped.

Old now, I feel I've paid my dues
to right behavior and
I pay less mind to the opinions
of others, but notice too,
that it's also true that
there is no one here
who cares.

Uncle Bushy's Farm

I remember the chickens walking around
aimlessly hunting and pecking at the ground
clucking their minds while the rooster crowed.

Pigs in their pen as we threw the slops over
taught me what the word 'wallowing' meant.

The odiferous barn was awash with the smells
of silage, fresh manure and hay, while I would
settle in to watch the cats so skillfully catch
the occasional stream of milk Uncle Bushy
would send their way.

I don't want to go back now.
I know it's 'better' there but
it's all machines now, and the cats
probably drink from a saucer while
no one opens the barn door to
usher the cows out to the pasture
accompanied by Rex, the dog.

My childhood town
(800 souls strong)
had its Village Idiot.

His name was Carl, and
he sat every summer afternoon
on one of the benches on
our two-block-long Main Street.

We children all respected Carl
(as was expected of us)
and when we passed by
we would all say
"Hello Carl!"
and Carl would answer us
with his only word,
"Lope"
and smile happily.

We children all learned
how important a smile was
and that a real idiot
would be anyone who
would not smile back at
our Carl.

The View From an Apple Tree (1936)

When I was a slip of a girl
I climbed the apple trees
that lined my block and
sat up among the apples
till mother called for lunch.

I could see everything from there
hidden in the green branches
with their tasty globes of red.
Puggy, the Colling's dog patrolling his yard.
Ardis Wilson hanging out her wash.
Monday was wash day all over town.
(The white sheets all hung on outer lines
and hanging in the middle, the household's
underwear and 'delicates' were
protected from the eye
of any passerby.)

The sidewalk down below my tree had cracks
and someone had dropped their roller skates
where they had fallen. A tricycle too, left out all night.

Across the lawn I watched the alley, home of
hollyhocks, lilac bushes and rhubarb which
came up like magic every year for rhubarb pie.
I watched for Vern Snow, who you could set your
watch by, my dad would say and sigh, for
Vern was getting old and blind and sick and
we all knew he'd someday die.
(Unlike my parents, I was sure.)

Sometimes a sound from farther down the alley would
presage a treat, and clip-clopping into sight would be
the drayman's horse and wagon.
The horse was old and swaybacked, and hauled things
to the dump so mother wouldn't let me hitch a ride,
but I could sometimes run to pet the horse's nose and
on the drayman's cue say, "Gee!"

So, I'm happy in my apple tree,
when I hear a screen door slam,
and Janie calling out,
"Come down and play.
I've got some brand new paper dolls."
So I put aside the book I'd carried up that tree,
and bite off Janie's bait and swallow Janie's hook
and climb down from the apple tree
to get a closer look.

The Noon Whistle
(West Concord, Minnesota, pop. 637) 1948

The noon whistle sounds from the top of the water-
tower and it's lunchtime all over town.

Kids hop on their bikes, mothers put Campbell
soup on the stove and spread peanut butter
on white bread while Erdman's Cafe on Main
Street fills up with bachelors and farmers in town
for the day.

A noon whistle in a small town can make a ritual
that marks a common life. It can be a compass
that even a small child can steer by.

Better than church bells on Sunday, than school
bells in the fall, it's daily, unfailing, reassuring.
The noon whistle leaves no one out.
A small town ceremonial moment that
connects us all.

Mother

When I was small, my
mother used to whistle.

Well, it wasn't exactly a whistle.
Not a real tune, either,
but a soft shusshing sound.

I would hear her shusshing
as she folded clothes or
folded the eggs into the flour and
I knew she was feeling happy.

The other day,
while watering my many potted plants,
I heard myself shusshing.
Startled, I was for a moment, I realized,
my mother.

Inside and Outside -- My Mother and Jim Harrison

This morning I sautéed some liver for breakfast.
Rather odd that, but I talked myself into it.
After breakfast I washed my hair and
soaked in the warm lavender scented water.
While listening to the rain on the roof,
I felt happy for the thirsty flowers in their
pots outside my front door.

Later on, it was while re-reading the poetry
of Jim Harrison, a man so often 'outside'
that I closed my eyes and thought about
being 'inside', and my mother.

My mother was a woman who,
in her Minnesota summers,
with her pitchers of lemonade and
her plate of molasses cookies would complain
as she passed through the back door to
join us on the lawn, would say,
"Why does everyone have to go OUTSIDE!"

A hothouse flower, my mother.
An inside girl who never knew Jim Harrison,
and wouldn't understand him if she had.

On Reading the Newspaper to a Resident of My Dad's Retirement Home in Zumbrota

The old lady licked her finger and used it
to lift a crumb off the table,
to put it back on her plate.
She is very old now, but
you can see she must have been pretty
in her day, though
clearly she doesn't care much
about that anymore.

She doesn't care much about
keeping up with 'issues' either
she tells me, or staying 'knowledgeable'.

All I seem to want now, she says, is
the local news, clean sheets,
a good cup of coffee like this,
with a treat and maybe a fresh flower
now and again to look at, to remind me.

I think to myself,
Is this, 'Nothing Lacking, Nothing in Excess'?

The Minnesota Old Folks Home

These days the elders talk of prescriptions, cataracts,
hearing aid malfunctions, the latest doctor visit and
the menu for tonight.

They used to talk about jobs, relationships, children; the
men, of sports, cars, and both genders, of vacations taken.

Only occasionally do the elders here enter the swamp
of regret, since the world of selective memory
is kind and erases much.
After all, bygones really are, now bygones.

You don't hear much about the future here, either,
so far down the slippery slope is this unsought rest.
It's pretty clear by this time too, that a person's
personal past doesn't interest others much,
and one's own world will pretty much die with one.

The men, in great old age, talk the least.
They are frail now, have nothing to do, and sit together
on the bench just outside the door.
They've just stopped talking altogether
their watery eyes stare blankly
at whatever passes by.

At the Rochester Airport

I remember my mother near her end.
Her skin was like fine silk
that would tear if touched.

I kept thinking as she walked toward me,
she's so small now, a little woman.
Where did she go?

She moved so carefully, so slowly,
as if she might break and suddenly,
I understood.

Seeing her, so changed,
made me catch my breath
as I walked toward her
across that hot tarmac,
wiping away a tear and
smiling my hello.

How long?

Hands

I look down now and see
at the end of my arms
my father's hands.

II
FRONT PORCH

Front Porch Lunch

Sitting in the shade of the crabapple tree,
  (a thousand pink globes ripening)
      I lunch.

On my plate, a big red tomato from the garden
  is resting on fresh basil leaves,
surrounded by white balls of mozzarella,
  all sprinkled with a vinaigrette.
    There is a toasted bagel spread
    with salmon cream cheese.
    A feast of plenty.

    I know this is a hungry world
    where people are still starving.
  Fruitlessly, I take a crust of my bread,
bow, and drop it in a bed of succulents,
    for all the hungry ghosts.

Front Porch (Undressing)

The tree in my front yard is
taking off its gorgeous golden dress
leaf by leaf.
Soon it will be bare-naked
(as we say in the Midwest).
Exposed will be its knobby joints and
crooked limbs to view.
Together we will wait for winter's white,
a new ermine-colored coat that we expect
will arrive soon,
by air.

Front Porch

Sitting on my front porch
 (Morning coffee, a cigarette)
I watch a cloud of local finches
 a massive flock
rise in the air before me.

They make a low humming sound
 a symphony of whirring wings,
 a thrilling overture before
  they settle on their
 separate chosen branches
  ready now to sing.

Expecting some melodic treat
  I have to laugh.
These frisky, fervent finches
  only give me
simple cheep, cheep, cheeps!

From the Front Porch (Snow)

In the beginning each urgent raindrop had to decide
whether to be snow or rain and
the lawn was only slightly dusted with white.

Within the hour all the drops had transformed.
Crystals of snow, clinging softly together,
fell slowly, lazily, until
each tree branch and twig
wore an inch of soft white cotton.

Our first winter snowfall!
A big comforter, spread wide and
fitting snugly.
Who could complain?

From the Front Porch to Arthur

The first storm of the season is coming and
there are gusting winds.
My lawn is sprinkled lavishly with gold.
I wish that I could name the tree that is
so abundantly giving up its leaves for my delight.
I have a friend, a poet, who knows the names
of almost all the trees and
I miss his company.
He would help me cap my sense of pleasure
in this tree-born treasure
with a name I could write down
as the title of this poem.

Lush green leaves

Lush green leaves everywhere and
just enough summer action to
watch from the front porch.
Skateboarders, dog walkers,
teenagers on their cell phones,
a toddler pushed in his stroller
by his dad, an old couple out
for their evening stroll.
Mary, the lamp lady, comes
to sit for a spell.
It's been a beautiful day we
tell each other
speaking the truth.

Su Tung-P'o

Sitting on the front porch
Reading Su Tung-P'o.
It's hard loving a Sung Dynasty poet
dead so long ago now.
On my cheek
a tear.

Summer Night

Summer Night - the midnight hour
scent of sprinkled cut grass, full moon
in silence deep and still, a thread of sound,
the distant freeway
what did I come out on my porch for?

Through my window I can hear that
   prizes are being awarded on
      the Boardwalk Beach.

"And the Number Six Award goes to...."
   followed by a roar from the crowd,
      followed by the sound of waves
         (nature's broom) sweeping the beach.

Then there is the rolling rhythm of the
   shrieks coming from the down and up
      of the distant roller coaster.

This, then, is the background music of so
   many summer days in Santa Cruz.
      It's so happy a thing, I would
         love to thank the composer.

One day the Bay is like a pewter dish
water and sky the same color.
On another, the Bay is robin's egg blue
dotted with bleached white sails
against a rosy gold sunset.
One never knows.

This effortless display of differences,
all equally fine,
is like turning the pages of
a Coffee Table Book
with sumptuous color plates.

It's hard to beat a walk to the beach.

My Redwood House

My wooden house,
    Board and batten redwood on
    the walls, the ceilings, the stairwell,
    is alive.

Each sun-warmed day will
    open all its pores and
    loosen all its joints.

Each cool dark night will
    close those pores so that
    my house will creak and
    stutter nervously.

It groans, breathes out and then
    breathes in, waking up my
    sleeping guests who wonder
    what they hear.

Is it an earthquake, an
    intruder on the stairs,
    a ghost?

Something there is
    in my redwood house.
    that remembers being,
    a tree.

It's a warm and sun-filled day in Santa Cruz.
    The radio announces storm waves coming from Hawaii
        I can see Steamer's Lane, a surf spot, from my study.

They will draw a crowd, these storm waves,
    white crested, huge,
        seductive, formidable,
            dangerous.

Black seals and grey sharks will swim below them,
    wet suits and surf boards on top.

On the surrounding crumbly cliffs there will be
    tourists and casting fisherman.

On the beaches there will be the playing children
    and the swimmers.

About the waves?
    Not everybody knows, or cares to know, but some of us
        will wait for the local news.

It's been years since I've been to the mountains
(if not because of cares, then because of illness)
I regret again, this year, the loss
of summer's mountain meadows,
Sierra's granite rock

—————————

The big round globe of gold
that hangs in tonight's sky
would have inspired Su Tung-P'o and his friends.
They saw it with Sung Dynasty minds
and wrote Sung Dynasty poems.

I have seen the moon on television and
watched a man walk on it.

Standing tonight in the sweet ocean air
of my California night, I too marvel.
I marvel at the moon's beauty.
I celebrate with them,
this free gift of nature.

Two More Walks

It's cold.
Today's waves are shivering up the beach
like white frosting on yesterday's cake.
Sky and water are both a sullen grey.
Across the Bay, the hills,
appear and disappear in the mist.
I, no dummy,
hurry home,
before the coming rain.

●

A bent old man who carries a cane
has stopped to pee.
He doesn't know I can see him
and I'm glad for that,
even though I suspect
he wouldn't care.

Age will trump self-consciousness
as some of us old ones forego
the world's rules, compelled by age
to make our own.

Winter Morning

A heavy fog last night.
The morning paper is wrapped in plastic.
The next-door cat is stepping high.
The slugs, fooled by the lack of sun have been slow
to take cover.
For a moment, I debate.
Slug poisons close at hand,
just there behind the garbage can.
But no.
I'll make my morning coffee, sweet elixir against the cold.
I'll open up my paper and read the news.
I'll leave the killing,
for another day.

Winter Day

An ocean wind, a rain-swept Sunday.
The birds have stopped flying.
The homeless cat has curled into a ball
        under the garden bench.
The tops of the trees are bending like grass.
There is a newly made river on the
        cluttered beach.
It's cold.
I am driven indoors,
        to make a soup,
        to put bread in the oven,
        to put wine in my glass, and
To count my blessings.

The calligraphy of bare black tree branches against
the grey winter sky
which is Salt Lake's seasonal art
no longer interests me. Now
I want plum blossoms, or
filigrees of tender green
against a robin's egg blue sky.
It's time to hang new art in
our universal gallery
which is known to offer
masterpieces
even to the unobserving, undeserving
public
every season still, for
free.

III
A RICH EXPERIENCE

Shock

We planned to meet at the local spa.
My husband, a space scientist
loved to swim

As I slid into the Jacuzzi, someone, a stranger
said to her friend, "I think that that man died."
And I knew.
I knew this was one of the moments when
everything changes.

Knowing, I moved now in slow motion. like swimming
through timeless, expanding space, and I thought,
I'm in shock. How odd.

When time stops, there is no self. When space
expands, we know as dream the tiny slice of
life we usually take for real.

Problem Solved

I pushed past the hands
trying to restrain me.
They meant well, but
I had to see him, even though
there were tubes still attached,
he was so recently dead.

I didn't know what it was I needed
until I saw him, my husband of thirty years,
space scientist, mathematician,
always tied to Mind, by his issues of
space, time, and zero.

Abandoned now in that small quiet room,
his eyes still open, he had a look I knew so well.
It was his look of discovery, of a problem
finally, suddenly solved, the 'Ah Ha' of
an equation worked out at last.
It was the look, his excited look,
just before he would turn to tell me....

He would have turned to tell me
this time too.

The house was a storehouse of memories.
The closet had his empty shoes and
    his suits still smelled of him.
His desk held his unpaid bills, his
        unfinished tax forms.
In the pantry were the last treats he bought
    Plum Pudding for him,
    Bailey's Irish Cream for me since
it was Christmas.

And on his bureau?
    Oh, my God
The leather European coin pouch,
All his old watches in the drawers,
the unused clean new handkerchiefs
    (he was meticulous) and
        in another drawer
a batch of his published papers,
        some awards,
            old pipes.

But, most of all,
    in the garage,
    it was his car,
(off base to ice cream-eating children)
    that did me in.
The car I drove home from the lot
    where he had parked it
        for the last time.

    How could he be gone?
He would have never left,
    Without his car.

Pillow Talk

I miss it.
I miss that time before sleep
at the end of each day
when all the little things,
like pebbles on our daily path
which have collected in our minds,
are dropped on our pillows,
before we move from the
dream which is each day
to the dreams we have each night.

Hospital Halls

I close the car door in the busy, noisy parking lot and
soon I'm walking down the long windowless hospital hall
where I grow quiet.

Passing the double elevator doors reserved for gurneys,
I pick up my pace,
for this is no place to dawdle, to linger, to relax.

These uncommonly clean and polished floors
have seen it all I realize.
This is the artery through which supplies are trundled.
The gauze, the linens, the tapes, the pills, and
all things surgical will pass through here
like blood passes through the tubes
inserted into a patient's arm
when needed.

Pain and fear and love and loss have also
walked these halls and left their
invisible traces, so that when you reach
the busy lobby, as I'm doing now,
you can feel things lighten up a bit.

And in the high ceilinged lobby there are
pots bursting with flowers and out the wide
front door real sunlight, a collie waiting patiently
for someone, and a flock of small birds chattering
up into a a sky so vast and blue that I too
feel the space and sense the shift of mind
so that I stand still for a moment.

I stand there, taking in the beauty of the world outside
which still is singing of creation myths and mysteries and
life and gratitude and then delight,
before I soldier on to see a loved one,
down yet another hall.

A Rich Experience

Hospital trips were hell.
To make it in and out of the car
without breaking a cancerous bone
was always a victory.
One time her doctor sent an ambulance
restraints and all, for just that reason,

Then, the long trip over the hill,
vomiting into the Mason Jar with its
new white lid, to keep the smell contained
between the heaves which numbered two,
or three, or more.

And after that the hours of transfusions,
blood for four or five, followed by Pemidronate
to keep her bones from breaking - another
two or three, depending.

She used to say that half way there,
still on the road, still vomiting, her
veins would 'catch on', say "NO!"
and start to close.
Smart veins, despair of all the nurses
with their intravenous tubes.

Her arms grew sore from all the punctures and
once she bled from every orifice, her
eyes, her nose, her gums, and even her vagina.
It can happen.

Your mouth can fill with blood, your
teeth turn red, which on top of those
bloodshot eyes is not a pretty picture.

Going home at last, she would laugh,
"Well, Mom, you can't say it isn't a rich experience!"

Hooked on Yoga

Stubborn, willful, and not one for
received wisdom, you were too quick for me,
too determined to see for yourself
the truth of things, to shine your own
searchlight on the world.

Outfoxed, I couldn't stop you.
Party hearty, drink and drugs, you
tried it all then stopped, done.
Settling on some favorites, your cigarette,
some weed, you turned to yoga next,
putting, as you said, to some good use
addiction's karmic seed.

It's in Her Bones, Now

I can feel myself disappearing
she says with a calmness
that is more than her 37 years.
Like an 80-year-old person
or a child with that curious disease where
age comes in fast motion.

She has always been fast.
Mind like a hummingbird, dazzled
and on to the next bright color.
It is her food. It's how she lives
Gobbling beauty.
Maybe she already knew as a child
she would need to fit it all in more quickly
than most. Not miss a minute
of her time on this juicy,
painful planet.

Now she wants to go slow.
She tastes her breath. She talks slower.
She does less and only
what she wants. Her ambition
has flared, aiming to reach 40
aiming now to notice
how the air touches her cheek, the kindness
of water, the sureness of earth
being somewhere to put our feet
and the blaze that lights
her body.

So she gets up each morning, fresh
before thought reminds her. Body
still breathing, through and beyond pain,
feeds herself foods that she loves,
and welcomes the whole mess
with her gaze.

When my dying daughter sleeps by day
a simple, elegant air of spaciousness
comes over her room.

Quiet stillness embraces everything
crows cawing above us,
surf murmuring on the beach below
barking seals, barking dogs.

There is the sweet chatter of children but
they are passing by and don't disturb.
Inside it is so quiet, so still, so big somehow
that there is room for life, room for death.

Like Light

She walked into a room like light,
Like fresh air, and we became
more interesting, more witty
when she was there.

A friend walked through the door of
the office where she worked, saw her
and said he could swear she radiated,
she made it brighter there.

Maybe dying early,
with your share of oxygen, of breath
compressed in time, your flame,
your life, becomes more bright, more full
and more inclined to shine.

Goneness

She did whatever it was she needed to do.
Whatever it was, and everyone
seems to agree, it is done.

Settled in like a cliff swallow, opened
her door to the wide waiting sea
and whatever else would come her way.

Closed it (when she needed to)
looked around and loved each thing
as it passed into her vision - and let it go.

When death came, that one too, she kept the
door open
though, who knows? The day before she died
she got out of bed, walked her frail body

over to that seaward-facing front door
and closed it. (She may have had a second thought about
leaving, wouldn't you?)

And now she is gone.

They say she's dead,
but I can't find dead

anywhere.

A Dream on the Anniversary
Of My Daughter's Death from Cancer

In my dream I am a failure.
It was my turn to make the meal.
People I cared about were there.
The main dish was undercooked and cold.
There was no wine.
I forgot dessert.

I rushed to a bakery in my dream,
hoping to find there, 'something', at least.
But I knew it would be too late.
My people would have gone.
Even the young boy, my helper,
turned away from me and disappeared.
There was no hope, no excuse.
No way.

Waking up it still seemed real.
It was my life and I had failed.
How sad.

Gradually, the morning sun
found its way into my room.
Sweet rapturous notes came from a nearby bird.
Excited children's chatter entered from the street below.
Eager seals began their barking on the distant wharf.
Beach waves spoke their song of come and go, come and go.
Suddenly, all of this was me, though
I was not all of this, and
again, the Way appeared.

How marvelous is each new day,
which starts all by itself,
so undeserved a gift.
How wondrous to be freed,
again and then again, by love.
Love of this world, this open space,
in which I do forever fail.

Going On

I want her companionship
and I can't have it.
She's dead,
though that's not quite the word.
She's in my mind, my memory of course.
(that old soporific
offered to the grieving).
It is not enough.

I can feel sorry for myself
and do, sometimes,
but then I hear her saying, impatiently,
"Mother, you know how you can indulge.
Don't! Just take care of yourself.
Just take care of life.
Just go on."

Something there is that
is not born and
does not die.

Robin

Ten years have passed since you left us,
    carried lifeless out the door.
The water sparkled in the Bay that day.
A black crow flying overhead seemed to
    announce that you were dead.
A life cut short, no time to finish a full term.
"So sad," most people said.

But wait, remember those long last days?
Still funny, honest, direct and fun, you were
    not sorrowful or even very sad.
Companioned by your friends you were just
    'present', enjoying what you had.

One day, while coming back from dreaded
    treatments, coping still with pain,
    acknowledging your coming end,
    you told your Mom that now, sans cure,
    with nothing left to do, you felt,
    and searching for the word, you said,
    "Complete."

Who could ask for more, when going to
    'the other shore'.
So we can happily chant, 'Bodhi Svaha'
    just like we did ten years ago,
    and remember how it was for us
    when we first saw you go.

Together

It could have been your footsteps on the stair
but isn't.
You could have been in that car stopping outside
but you are not.
The telephone rings
but you are not calling,
as you used to do all those mornings when
you were dying
and I'd go over to bring you your breakfast,
open your curtains,
air your room
freshen the flowers,
start whatever day
we had left
together.

Again

I almost daily offer incense, happily
light a candle over her ashes and
then sit down and face the wall.
But these are more dangerous days.
Her anniversary draws near.
The ocean off her cliff begins to swell,
with grief, so that I find its salty tears
are here, running down my cheeks,
again.

The Changeling

She will never grow old
my mischievous, changeling child,
the laughing child, the student,
who became an efficient working woman
just to see if she could do a nine–to-five
and showed up next
as a cancer patient.

She had grown wise
and used all she had learned
in her 31 years
to meet each of the days
in her remaining six
while holding death's hand.

Life moves on
in its unstoppable way,
and now I am the one
who grows old.

Peter

He was the one who called 911
    the day his dad,
    sitting at the oak desk,
    had a heart attack.
He was the one who drove with me,
    the day his dad,
    swimming at the spa,
    had his last attack, his last ambulance ride,
    and lay there, in the hospital, dead.
He was there when I packed,
    the day before I
    had my breast cut off,
    and sent him back to school
He was the one we called,
    the day his sister
    got her diagnosis –
    cancer, too.
He was the one who sat with
    his dying sister,
    on her cliff,
    whenever he could.
Oh, and I forgot,
    he was the one who dug the grave
    for Duffy, beloved family dog.
And the day he got married,
    he was the one whose voice broke as he
    repeated, "In sickness and in health,
    till death do us part."

A Short History After Down and Out in Sunnyvale
-- for Peter

Funeral over, a widow now.
Ashes still on the bedroom bureau,
the rapist crawls in the small, high bathroom window.

There was a trial.
It was a 'performance piece' in a courtroom
full of cops, guns, and leather
with lawyers in expensive Italian shoes.

Still stressed and with no pension, no Social Security and
two children still in college,
I painted the house for sale and
packed to move.

After another and necessary move to Santa Cruz,
(48 boxes to pack and Starving Student for furniture)
it was cancer next.
After weeks of radiation and still healing, it was
cancer for your sister too.

So, some long years of support for Robin through
her horrendous treatments and, while she was
dying, operations for me too (two hernias, cataracts),
and then her death with death's duties to attend to.

After all of that, there was nowhere to go but 'up',
and not much left to fear beyond more of the same.
Practiced now, I knew there was no choice but,
'Going on...Going on...Going on. . .

A Family Poem

My daughter-in-law plays the harp
I know nothing about the harp
(I should add, very little about any instrument)
But, I am sitting now in a modern mountain church and
I am waiting for her solo with the Chamber Orchestra
It is number 111 on the program

There is a large two-story window in this church
Beyond the glass, a wild-flowered meadow, sun drenched
        mountains
Inside, like me, the audience has settled in
The orchestra plays Respighi, then Prokofiev

It is her turn now
She takes her seat, the conductor raises his baton
Ah! this moment
The moment before a performance begins
That tear in time
One foot in the old world, the other not yet down
There is the possibility of falling
One holds one's breath

The music begins, and Debussy and Louise
Obviously old friends in perfect collaboration
Lift me from my wooden pew
Float me out that church window on a rainbow of sound
Where I breathe the mountain air
Where I inhale deeply, the Gift of Art

Back in my solid pew
Debussy and Louise now done with me

I applaud with the others, then
Turn to my son, and realize
There are tears on my cheek

As I said, I know nothing about the harp
I know even less about musical instruments or Debussy
But I do know a lot, now, about my daughter-in-law
Who is the musician, Louise

The Visit

My beloved boy, now
            a man,
has left, after a visit, but
happiness still lingers here.
He's left some behind
in this, his Mom's house.

They Have Gone

I wander through the winter's sun-bright empty rooms that
my loved ones
have left and
now, in the new quiet, and
without an agenda, I'm empty too, and
sad.

So, I fill the washer with bathroom towels
and soiled sheets.

Next, I put away the leftovers,
clean the kitchen counters,
put the wine bottles in the trash,
vacuum the rugs and
arrange fresh flowers.

Then, I take a bath with lavender suds and soap,
and take a nap, knowing,
that though I'll miss them still,
when I awake, like my house
I'll also be restored.

This old routine is a trick I play
on myself.
It always works.
Better than a drink, a pill, a movie.
It's just doing what you should do.
One of the four kinds of happiness.

IV
PLEASE TAKE GOOD CARE OF YOURSELF

Red-tailed hawks have arrived from
the Sierras.
There are plump squirrels here.
Crows sound the alarm.

I'm neutral, I understand.
Everyone needs to eat.

The little bonus of my day is this,
though I can hear the action,
I do not see, the act.

Tongue

I have a big tongue in a pot on the stove.
Soon I will cool it and
peel off its taste buds and
slice it for lunch.

Should we know where our food comes from?
Well, I grew up loving cows and
have looked fondly into many a big brown eye,
but not today.
Today I eat what I love.

The Dog I Will Never Have

I am looking for a name
for the dog I will never have,
the one who will want to sleep
on my bed, curled up like a furry ball
that circles slowly before it
settles into place.
I'm at a loss.

My dog, I think, is small and
doesn't drool or bark unless
it's overcome with joy or
asking to go out. Good Dog!

We will be companions,
just hanging out together.
Together while I clip the edges of the lawn.
Together in the kitchen, source of so much doggy joy.
Together in the car and on the street.

They say a dog should have a name
that's good for 'calling' in the park, and there should be
a hard consonant somewhere in that name. Who knew?
That knocks out Zeus but leaves in Rover,
but neither, it seems, will do.

Oh, how to name a dog I do not have, and
do not feed, or pet, or walk, but disappointed
only feel the loss, the loss....

Rain on the Roof

If there is a better sound
  than rain on the roof,
  I don't know it.

Today's soft, steady, fresh spring rain
  is punctuated by a splash
  whenever a car passes through
  the puddled street below.

I put down my book to listen,
  present to the rain, so sweet,
  and think of all the other times,
  so many now.

My mother used to tell me that
  the trees could drink and
  wash their leaves and that was why
  they were so happy
  in the rain.

I am happy too, for
  I am washed with pleasure by
  the sound of the rain
  on the roof.

Proper Worship

The first rain of a California winter is the best rain.
We've been waiting for so long.
Dusty leaves, dry earth, shrunken reservoirs
and my thirsty flower pots
whose water comes from a garden hose
and not from heaven.

In Minnesota we had cisterns
to catch the summer rain which
sometimes came with thunder
and lightening on our plain.
But we could have our floods.

In California we all watch for winter rain
which makes the lion-colored hills
turn green again and cools the air enough
so people leave the sandy beach
in favor of a nook, and in my case a book.
We too, can have our floods.

Water is earth's life blood, a wonder,
our recurring need, our miracle,
a gift for all of us, so undeserved.
So how did we forget to worship water?
Where are our Water Temples?

Just like an ice cube melts in anybody's hand,
our awareness of water has melted away,
and we are in danger.

We look now in the hope it's not too late,
to the Government,
to policy makers,
to remember the rain and to
give it its sacred due.

On Not Going Out

Trees sway together in the wind
Wild grasses bend down weighed with the rain
          Big waves pound the beach
There will be no moon climbing over the Bay
                    tonight.

I could go for my therapeutic walk, but I'd
              rather take a nap.
                Like the Sun,
              I won't go out.

Widowed now and living alone,
this is what I saw as
I came down the stairs to
make my morning coffee.

I saw the Alstroemeria on the living room coffee table.
I saw the Oriental rug I cross on my way to the kitchen,
the red cup I always use.

Then, fresh coffee in hand and on my way back, to the
front door, for the morning papers,
finally,
I saw him, a complete stranger, a man,
sound asleep on the living room sofa!

So, I opened the door.
I called out firmly,
"Wake Up, Wake Up"
and
"Leave, Leave, Just Leave."

Murmuring as he put on his shoes,
"I'm so sorry, I'm so sorry.
You are a nice lady."
He was gone.

To the Poet Elizabeth Bishop

Your famous line, "The art of losing isn't hard to master,"
is true.
It's also true that it's the art of 'letting go' that's hard.
Losing, after all, just happens, and
answers to a will that's not our own
like lightning strikes or hurricanes,
there is no choice.

Letting go, is choice itself.
One must discriminate, and choice becomes the thing to
master, for we can close our doors against all signs
of slowly changing weather and draw close
our homemade patchwork quilts,
made up of all that is familiar,
in fear that letting go is only self-inflicted loss.

After all, which long held opinions could we do without?
What self-defining habits, attitudes, responsibilities,
indeed of all we've put together, gathered to us,
making up that precious fiction, our identity,
could we let go, would we let go, and
here's the rub,
who would we be
then?

Now

Women and children are being raped in the Sudan
They must choose each day
who among them will go
beyond the safety of the camp
for firewood - a Sophie's choice.

Here, in California, I am able
to change the channel to
    a gardening show
        a cooking show
            a movie
Viewing it all from the comfort
of my green chair.

What has happened to time and space?
The pressing of a button puts these worlds
together in a dream beyond knowing
    how we are to think
        how we are to feel
            what we are to do,
              Now.

I Smoke

I've always had a love of smoke!
Campfire smoke from red coals
    surrounded by dark woods
        of black and green pines.

I smell the soil of the tobacco fields in smoke.
    All fields really, and
        the earth that supports us all –
            the dirt.

I sense the nature of all the grasses,
    of all the tree barks,
        the leaves that cover the forest floor,
        of tundra.

Rolling Thunder said you just
    had to respect and honor
        the tobacco you smoke.

My friends all seem to say,
    you just have to
        quit.

I 80 Road Trip (Reno to Salt Lake)

Going East out of Reno,
I 80 follows the Truckee River.
Cottonwoods line its banks.
Mountains ring the horizons.
The road is a gray ribbon which will
unfurl ahead for the next seven hours.

It's eight thirty in the morning when we start.
The sun's at ten o'clock.
There is not a cloud in the sky.
Off road, thermal vents are steaming.
There is silvered light in the far distance,
 the stuff mirages are made of.
 They get no rain out here.

Road signs flash by and we seem to drift through
wide open space, the space of buff colored land and
big empty sky, the iconic space of the West.
Our speed evokes a drifting, minimalist way of
seeing, à la Philip Glass. Just layered repetitions of
desert views as the landscape empties out.
No people, no buildings, only sagebrush,
Mesquite, and once in a while some piñon pine,
some black-eyed Susans.

All I 80 towns are 'off-road' here.
There is a ghost town called Chicken Creek.
Lovelock has a prison.
Battle Mountain has gold mines still, though
Time magazine has called it
"the armpit of America."

Winnemucca sports a road sign that reads,
"Butch Cassidy left here rich and so can you."
Hours later, when the Humboldt River surprises
us with green fields, there is the off-road town of
Elko where cowboy poets gather once a year
to speak their truth to fans.

Going into Wendover we begin to see
the vast salt flats, and soon huge mounds of
shimmering white salt line the road on the left.
On the right, big gray mounds of copper tailings
from the Kennecott mines appear.

Then, at last, the Wasatch Range is dead ahead with
Salt Lake at its base.
I 80 will go on, but we will not.
For now, this is space enough.

If you ever have 'cabin fever',
if you've ever been 'cooped up' or city-stressed,
if you feel a need for 'space',
there is a perfect antidote available –
The American Road Trip, Reno to Salt Lake.

The Daily Life of God

Don't you wonder about
  the daily life of God?
Does he have toast or miso soup or
  eggs or even gruel for breakfast?
Or has he given up eating altogether,
  subsisting on rainbows, worshipful vibrations
  strained through a gossamer mesh to
  keep all selfish pleading, like rocks, out?
Does he have any friends beside his poor son
  and, I guess, his virginal wife? Because
  worshipers aren't friends, aren't peers,
  and can be very boring, I'm sure.
And about that throne.
  God is pretty old now, and I hope
  that all that gold has been padded
  so that it's truly comfortable,
  with maybe wheels, to help him
  get around,

Seventy-One

I'm seventy-one this year and I still don't know
what it means to grow old.

Is it the need for a nap, for glasses, pills, or
is it the greater number of doctors appointments?
Is it the loss of strength, a less reliable sense of
balance, the death of old friends? Or, is it none of
the above...

This morning's zazen brought me the soft 'hooo' of
a distant barn owl and in a moment, I was seven
again and snug in my mother's fresh sheets -
listening...
I could smell the sweet prairie air of summer, of
a warm Minnesota morning.

How old am I really?
I know when I'm sick or sad or in pain.
I know when I'm afraid or happy,
but I don't know how old I am.
Is that the reason we humans learned
to count? So we could pretend to
know how old we are and
CELEBRATE!

Seventy-Four

Am I dissolving, disappearing
    into the universe
        bit by bit?
So much of what I used to think of
    as myself
        is gone.
Who knows where?
    A mystery
        I think.

Friends say it's aging,
    Is that what
        this is?

As for me, I only know
    what it feels like
        these days
It feels like being undressed
    very slowly
        and very gently
by my mother.

Seasons

Everything has its season it is said, and
mine ended some time ago,
I suppose one could say.

I can't complain, even though
I feel, perhaps, rather like
an over-ripe fruit.
And though I know that
there are a few spots of decay,
I still know the sweetness
that comes with 'ripe', and
there is compensation enough
in that, for a life that still
tastes good.

Ruins

I live in a ruined house
grateful for life
but wary of death.
Not groveling before it,
not nervous, but respectful
now that parents, husband,
daughter, so many friends
and even pets
have gone that way.

Ruins are great teachers.
Ruins tell the tale of time
and death and change and of the need
to pay attention to each moment
while it lasts, for the present
is where our life is lived.

Road Signs

There is a trio of signs I see whenever I lift my
eyes from a book and glance out my window.

The first sign reads, NOT A THROUGH STREET.
Rather philosophical that.
I muse awhile and then decide
I'm just glad it doesn't say,
DEAD END.

The second sign reads, REDUCE SPEED,
In my case, at 74, it's a 'done deal'.
(An ongoing process, not a virtue.)

The third signs reads, NEIBORHOOD WATCH.
and in smaller type, which I had
to venture out in the street to read,
"Program in force. We immediately report
all suspicious persons and activities to our
Police Department.'

To me, that brings it all home.
So, if a man without a face, who
is dressed in a black cape with a hood
and carrying a scythe, should be stalking
around my neighborhood?
He is going to JAIL!
He won't make it to my house,
I'm happy to say.

Regret

I tried to find him once
some fifty years after I left him
without explaining.
We were kids then really, though he had finished law,
and I was still in college.

I know I hurt him,
my mother told me.
He had come to her and cried,
to see if she could help,
could tell him where I was or why,
but I was half a continent away by then and
truly gone, for I had run away from him.

It took me fifty years to know
why he had differed from the rest,
to remember what I'd loved and feared.
He helped me grow back then. Grow
from a girl 'in love' with a boy,
to a woman who loved a man.
No small thing.

I wanted to apologize I think,
for truly he deserved much more from me.
Repentant after all those years I wanted him to know,
it wasn't him I didn't love so many years ago but
young, confused, afraid, bereft of words,
the problem was with me.
I couldn't wrap my mind around his future life.
I couldn't bear to be, a lawyer's wife!

Well, I couldn't find him after all.
He may be dead, who knows.
And that long silence still remains
a testament to time and the sad truth
that truth, however difficult it seemed
would have been the way to go.

With images of time and place,
preserving silence still,
I found a way to meet him if only in my mind.
Going beyond reality I fantasized a scene
that would make my late life wish come true.

My hero now is seventy-eight, thin but seems quite spry.
He's witty still, and warm, intelligently wry.
Amused to hear my story he will use his cane to cross the
room and happily sit down with me.
He'll pour some wine to toast us both.
We'll eat Contentment Pie.
He'll laugh with me as we reflect
from our aged vantage post,
that love's 'falling together' in youth can be good, and
seems to serve some kind of test, but
'falling apart' is a part of life too, and is sometimes
all for the best.

Poor Me

Swollen and sick,
I creep into bed and pull the covers close
for warmth,
for sinking into sleep so deep,
so fertilized with dreams
that waking I can barely make my stumbling way
to where nasturtiums bloom
outside my kitchen door.
The flowers of the poor.

Organic Recital

I had a blood test that
pronounced my basic organs
and my brain still sound.
This is the kind of news
that one likes to hear
at eighty.
A nurse friend calls it
"The Organ Recital."

I'm happy there is no need
for all those glasses of water
before a colonoscopy,
no need for the wheel chair, and
most of all,
no need to accept the kindness of strangers
because I no longer remember
the way home.

Maybe

Maybe I'll become
  really old
Instead of
  just old.

Maybe more of the
  people I love
    I'll lose.
After all, why not?

I could still decide to travel
  to far places
    but I doubt it.

Will I lose my love
  of daily life?
    Probably not.

I walk through each season still,
  making the most of them
    while they last.

Spring light,
  Summer's fog,
    Fall's leaves.

The seasons are like chapters in a book
  I can't put down
    yet.

I can understand why we project
a heaven where loved ones await us.

How scary if, on the 'other side'
there might be no one, or
no one one knows.

Would God be enough?
What if it was empty there,
even of him?

First Stop in My Afterlife Trip

Here is where I will go first when I die.
To Hangzhou in the Lower Yangtze Region
of China and to the renowned soft beauty
of the West Lake there.

I will meet up with Su Tung-P'o who will be
among the scholar-gentlemen and pleasure-
loving monks who have come down to the
lake from the villas, temples and pagodas
that ornament the surrounding hills.

It is the eleventh century and groups of
literati are going out on the pleasure-seeker
boats to eat well, to drink wine poured by
sing-song women and to make poems.

I will bring Kobun along since I know he loves
Su Tung-P'o too, and together we will make a
guest list for the large gargoyle-headed boat
we will engage – the one with the expert cook.

Since we are, all of us, 'dead', there is no problem
with either time or space for us, but if you are
living, we must wait for you.

There is a lot to be said for a poetry party with
Su Tung-P'o and friends on a warm spring day on
West Lake, so it's best to sign up now.

Another Age

I've been another age for some time now.
        My house is weathered.
Younger friends, sick with love still
        come together, fall apart,
and show their faith in time, time for
        reconstruction.

I, no longer side-by-side with any other,
        find old passions
        don't disturb me.
They've run away into the woods.

Love remains, though different now.
More like the softly spreading night fog
        or like the early moonlight
leaking through the cracks in this old cottage
        lighting up the rooms.

Parinirvana Sutra

"I think he's dead," she said.
It was a middle-of-the-night telephone call.

The caller was his wife.
His wife who hated hospitals,
who wouldn't go near any funeral ever, anywhere,
and who was panicked now.

I threw on some clothes,
called Kobun, my Zen teacher,
told my husband to check the sleeping children,
and follow me if he could.

It was so dark and so very quiet
in that late night neighborhood that
the only sounds came from our three cars
as we parked and gathered in his small house.

Careful not to waken the sleeping neighbors,
glad for the cover of that moonless night,
I wandered the lawns searching for a sprig of pine
for the ritual to come while
back inside the only lighted house his
wife had emptied her cut glass sugar bowl so we
could fill it with the water the long-needled pine
would sprinkle around the room for
Buddha, Dharma, Sangha.

After his nervous, exhausted wife asked
if she could lie down
just outside his room,
my husband and I took our places

on one side of his gurney,
(his home for many years)
while Kobun, on the other side,
after looking deeply into those
still open eyes,
opened his Sutra Book,
and began to chant.

It takes a long time to chant
the complete Parinirvana Sutra.
Time enough to settle down with death.
Time to ride the chant to death's stillness,
to acceptance, to the end.
And by the end, his eyes had closed
all by themselves.

In the adjoining room, his wife, calm now too,
inquired as we rejoined her,
"Kobun, what was that strange long chant?"
Kobun answered, "Buddha's words to people
around him when he died."
"Well", she insisted, "What did Buddha say?"
And Kobun answered,
"I'm going away now.
Please take good care of yourself."

An Old Friend

I have a pot that's an old friend.
I've had it for at least forty years.
I make winter soups in it, chili, and
my dead mother-in-law's stew at least
once a year.

My pot has lacked one handle,
lo these many years, but
stainless steel doesn't wear out
at the same rate I do and
it still 'fits the bill'.

I call my pot, "Sweetheart" when
I lift it down from its high shelf each fall.
No one is there to hear me being silly.
Old woman gone daft . . .
talking to her pots.

V
ZEN FOOTPRINTS

I make it a habit now, to sit in my study
and watch the sun set.
From my study window I see
the beach and the Bay, bathed in color,
the fog moving in,
the last of the tiny figures
still strolling below me
before night falls.
I think of all I love about this place.

•

Since my spine started telling me
that it was wearing out, I paid attention, and
understood my newfound interest in all benches
and my love for my old green chair.

•

At seventy five, I'm losing eyebrow hair and lashes
but suspect they have not gone too far,
and reappear now, on my chin.

•

My son washed my floor and cut the grass and shopped.
My daughter-in-law vacuumed, cleaned and straightened and
    shopped.
They have prepared me for an operation
How can I not recover, feeling so loved, so cared for.

Home again I hear the mockingbird
and remember my dad.
Sitting in his lawn chair
he composed new melodies
for them to sing.

•

That college girl praying so many years ago
in her college dorm's chapel,
that was me,
talking to myself.

•

Two morning papers,
coffee on the chair arm.
No obligations for the day?
This I know, now, is luxury.

•

I have my favorite pen.
It's named Precise,
which I'd love to be.

•

Today, I lost my patience,
a not uncommon occurrence.
It doesn't feel as good as
finding it again, along with my breath,
where it hangs out.

Now that I can walk again,
I take a late night stroll
and standing on my cliff I see,
how moonlight has filled the Bay.

●

My pleasures?
Today it's a good book.
Yesterday a poem.
Tomorrow a long walk.

●

Against the sky, birds bob and weave.
White waves decorate the beach.
By now I know the charm of each cliff-top view.
I stop wherever it seems best
and breathe the ocean air.

●

Partings and reunions.
Joys and sorrows.
Tears and laughter.
Having had it all, I can't complain,
As my hair grows white.

Today I felt an autumn wind and
the sun's weak rays.
An overgrown orchard hid its last lemons
beside a desolate hillside path
that had no walkers.
Winter is just over that hill.

●

My ten-year-old car,
which I hosed off today,
shined up, happily,
expecting to go out at last.

I'm sitting at the kitchen table when
the mouse and I lock eyes.
Only the room moves.

•

The fevered baby cries
The cool rain on the roof
cannot reach him.

•

Our dog barks and
then is silent
waiting for a reply.
Hearing none he turns
and comes inside.

•

A spring storm.
High winds gusting.
Though it's deep night
the house wakes up,
creaks and shakes while
I close its windows.

Having accepted all
this year's spring rain
the San Lorenzo river
rushes to the Bay

•

A steep path winds down
the succulent-covered cliff
to the windswept beach
a lone swimmer
braves the waves

•

Tired from a walk
I sit for a long moment
refreshed by the vastness
of the ocean view

•

Once in a while I hear
floating in on the evening fog
the muffled bark of a seal

•

In light from the setting sun
shining through the leaves
I see the many shades
of summer

Awakened by the courtship
of the chattering birds
Still, I drift back to sleep
Dreaming of Spring

•

Tucked between cottages
a small garden
pregnant with summer
bursts into bloom

•

Watching the day fade
I turn to go home
with one last look
at the pink sky

•

Patiently sitting
outside the Post Office
the blind old dog's nose
waits for his master's smell

•

Somehow I ended up
living here above the Bay
the seasons pass
as do the years –
　　　but who keeps track?

Some Potsherds and Tumuli from 2008 Dig Site

Philosophers loitering on the cliff debate
whether Santa Cruz is a location or
a state of mind

•

I know the big black crow
landing outside my window
is just as surprised
to see me

•

Made for each other
the hole in my favorite slipper
and duct tape

•

The chance that my nude body
will give anybody a thrill
has vanished
but I find that my body
no longer cares

•

Birds and squirrels balancing precariously on
the telephone wire
Don't ring me up!

Old women fish for compliments
by mentioning their age
It works

•

My children sometimes lived
with two demented adults
That they survived speaks well
for miracles

•

Unplanned obsolescence
describes most
elders

•

No one talks about the pleasure of
forgetting
I would, if I could remember it

•

I'm not at the end of my rope
but I notice now
it's frayed

•

I love waking up
I love going to sleep,
sometimes too,
the hours between

I think I understand the economic
                        downturn
            but I said the same thing about
                        fractions

                              •

Cheers to all those Midwesterners
                    who never let the gas go below
                        half a tank

Therapy

Assigned as physical postoperative therapy, a daily
therapeutic walk, I manned my big-wheeled walker
and, in order to stay encouraged promised to jot
down a line or two on returning. A kind of, 'Exercise
Plus', to make it more enjoyable:

Sparkling through the green leaves,
today's sun.
The nearby oak however, is starting to turn.
Some yellow leaves, some red.
Today's sharp wind
breathes the freshness of an early chill.
I can feel the season turning.

•

Walked eighteen blocks before noon.
Refreshed my kitchen windowsill
with flowers gleaned on the way,
I just pick little flowers, ones that
are hanging off a fence, or over a sidewalk.
(Ones that won't be missed?)
I'm a happy thief today.

•

Gone is the mad chatter of spring birds.
There is no warm summer breeze.
Still, I can enjoy a cold, clear day
of colored leaves, if followed by
a hot cup of soup.

Today the clouds are pure white cotton balls
in a baby blue sky.
Far across the dark blue Bay I can see
the misted mountains behind Monterey, but
here, clamoring for my attention,
some bright, bold, yellow Zinnias.
Beauty everywhere.

●

Picking fall grasses
I forget the time,
and linger too long
on this path of
newly noticed things.

●

Exhausted by this windy walk
I found a cliff-side bench
from which to watch the cormorants.
Funereal figures.
All facing into the wind like me,
They seemed so apropos an image
I had to laugh.

●

Flowers and trees all know
that fall is in the world.
I can see life taking cover,
its force diminishing with
the paler sun.

The rains are due soon in California.
The brick beyond my gate
will grow its velvety green moss.
Now, I will celebrate my red chrysanthemums.
They blossomed just last week.
Why be impatient?
Each thing has its season.
Even me.

●

The Princess Hibiscus petals
cover the sidewalks all over
my neighborhood.
I walk on purple.

●

The big, fat, blue bellied fly
that came home with me today
is washing his hands on the
windowsill above my sink.
I told him he had five minutes
and then I opened the door.
He heard me and left.
They will do that sometimes
and it's worth a try.

Unconcerned with ceremonial matters
the drifting raft
sans sails
still crosses over
to the other side

Already knowing
there is no attainment
Still, surprised,
at so much to lose,
we go on

To be with,
that's the Way
Realizing enlightenment
without being aware of it
is just as Dogen says
Doing nothing special
not even trying -
Bodhi-Mind

The dog passing by
doesn't want rebirth
tail wagging, head up,
he's on his way
And you?

Only on our last bed
Is it easy to see
Worldly gain and losses
Are empty

The returning fog
Already knows
My house

Made in the USA
San Bernardino, CA
24 May 2016